Tunes You've Always Wanted To Play

Easy Classics for

violin

with Piano Accompaniment
Arranged by Jack Long

CHESTER MUSIC

(A division of Music Sales Limited)
8/9 Frith Street, London W1V 5TZ

This book © Copyright 1997 Chester Music
Order No. CH61292 ISBN 0-7119-6687-7
Music processed by Enigma Music Production Services
Cover design by Pemberton & Whitefoord
Printed in the United Kingdom by Caligraving Limited, Thetford, Norfolk

CONTENTS

ANDANTE CANTABILE

from String Quartet Op.3 No.5

F. J. Haydn

Andante cantabile

poco cresc.

mf

mf

mf

MARCH OF THE MEN OF HARLECH

Alla marcia
poco stacc. e sempre marc.

Welsh Air

WALTZ

from Coppelia

L. Delibes

PLAISIR D'AMOUR

G. Martini

Moderato

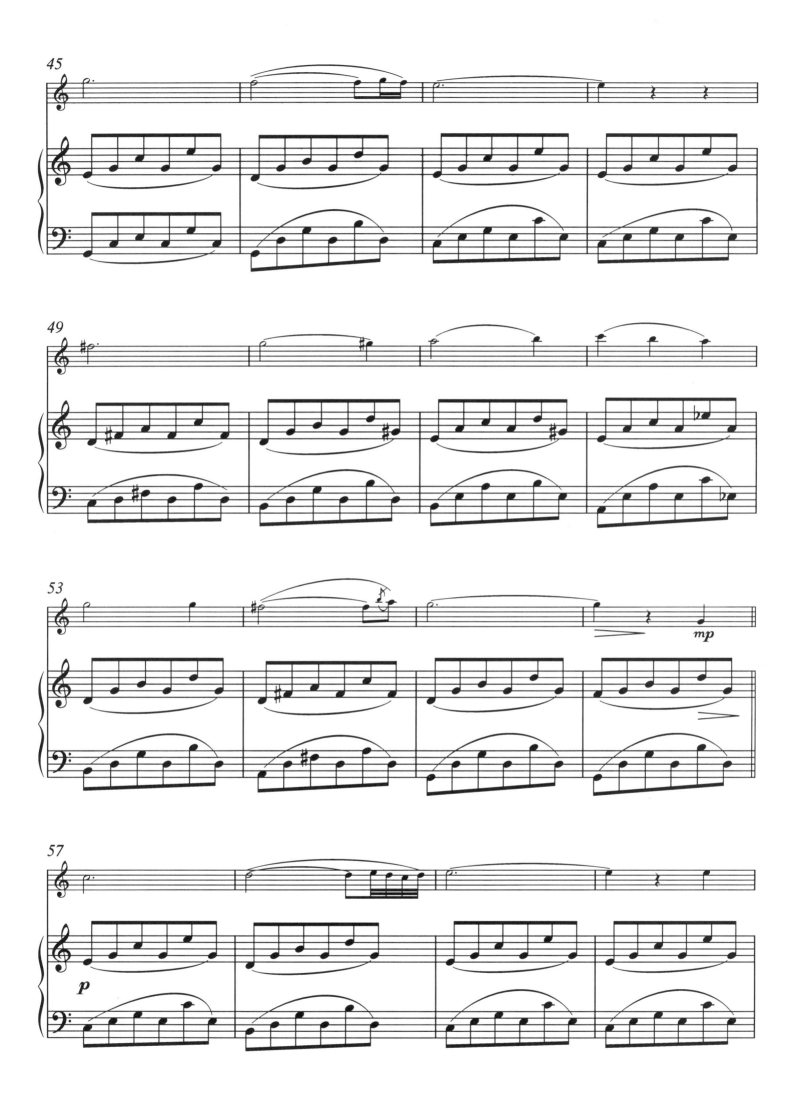

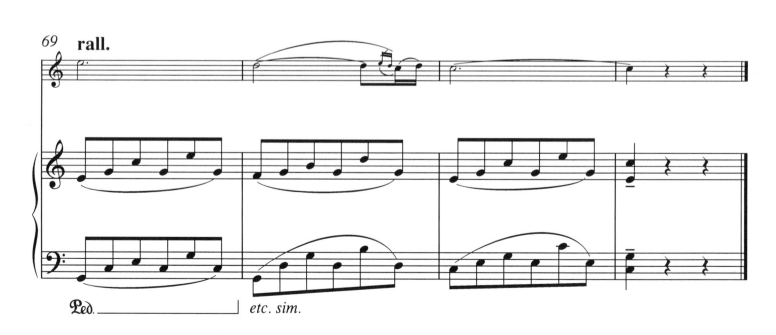

THEMES FROM ROSAMUNDE

F. Schubert

THE LONDONDERRY AIR

Irish Air

THEMES FROM THE FOUR SEASONS

Moderato

A. Vivaldi

1. Spring

2. Autumn
Più mosso

poco a poco dim.

poco a poco dim.

24

WHAT IS LIFE?

from Orfeo ed Euridice

C. W. Gluck

Andante espressivo

AIR ON THE G STRING

from Suite No.3 in D

J. S. Bach

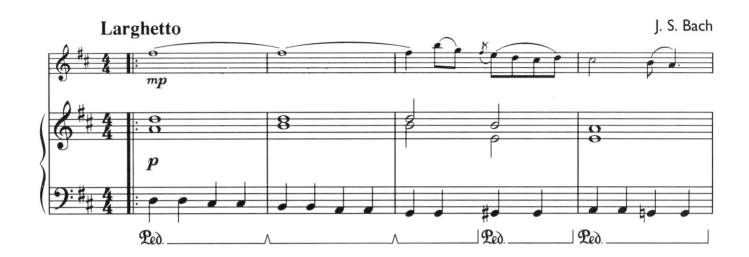

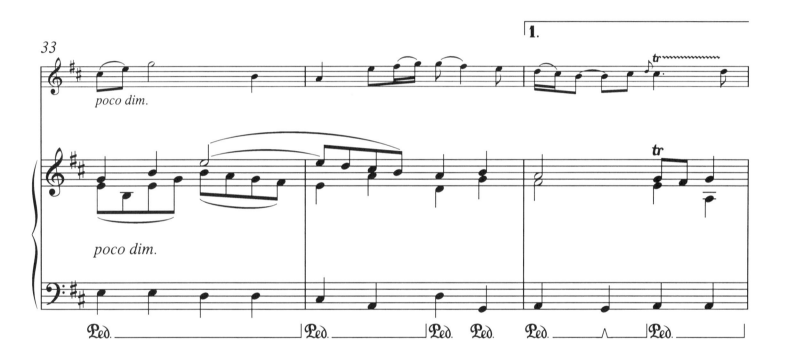

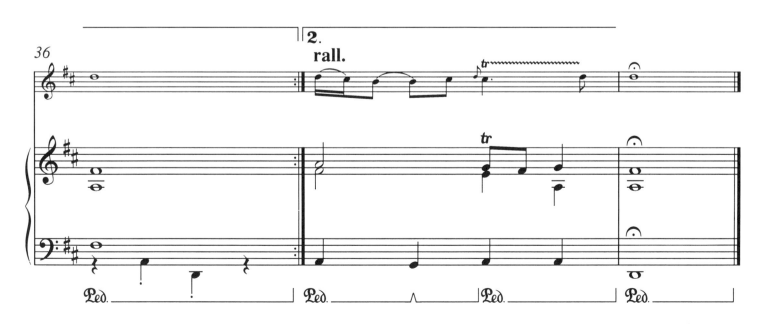

BARCAROLLE

from Tales of Hoffmann

J. Offenbach

SCOTLAND THE BRAVE

Scottish Air

MINUET IN G

L. van Beethoven

Andante

To  Coda

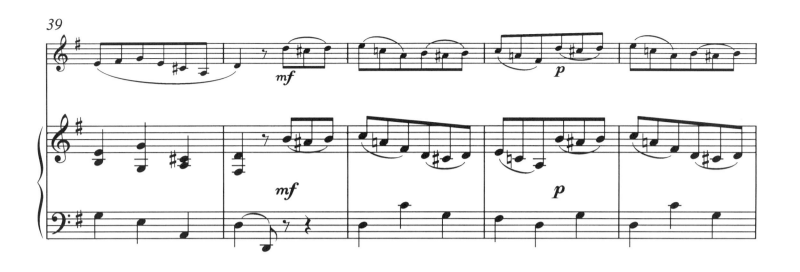

ANDANTE CANTABILE

from Quartet in D Op. 11

P. Tchaikovsky

Andante cantabile

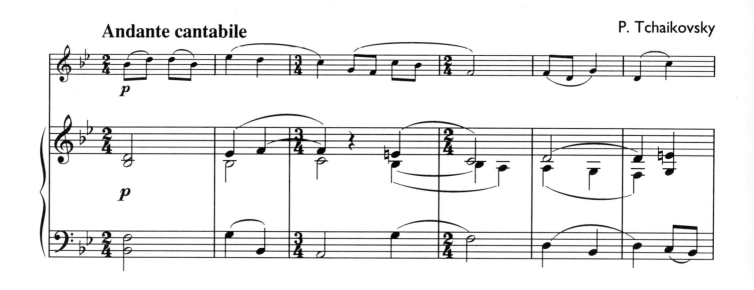

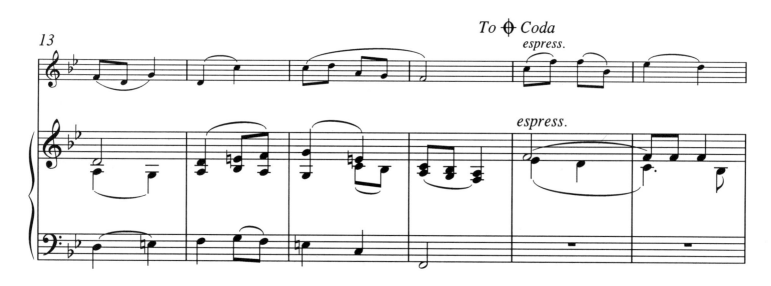

NOCTURNE

from Quartet No. 2 in D

Andante espressivo

A. Borodin

poco rall.

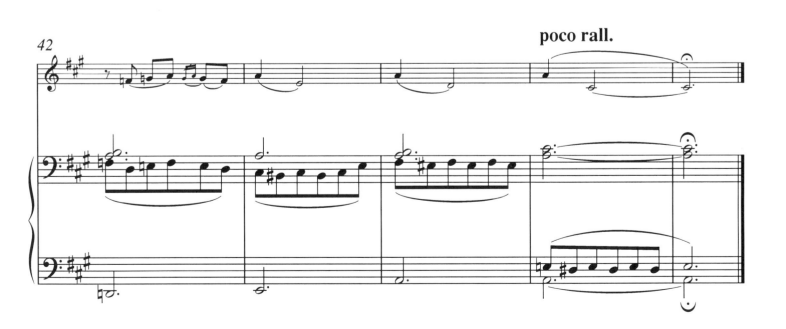

GREENSLEEVES/LOVELY JOAN

Andante sostenuto

English Airs

MINUET

Moderato e grazioso

L. Boccherini

To Coda
(2nd time)

MAZURKA

Op. 7 No. 1

F. Chopin

NORWEGIAN DANCE

Op. 35 No. 2

E. Grieg

SPRING SONG
Songs Without Words, No. 30

F. Mendelssohn

Allegretto grazioso

FLOWER DUET

from Lakmé

L. Delibes

Andantino con moto

MEDITATION

from Thaïs

J. Massenet

Andante religioso

70

THEMES FROM EINE KLEINE NACHTMUSIK

W. A. Mozart